DAY OF THE

ELEPHANTS

The True Story of Lives Lost
in Liberia and Found in America

Ron Swager

&

Ed Chinn

http://coolriverpub.com

ISBN: 978-0-9830214-6-9

Printed in the United States of America

When bull elephants fight,
the grass always loses.

African Proverb

TABLE OF CONTENTS

ACKNOWLEDGMENTS

Ron Swager

I never believed I would write a book until that Friday in May 2011 when Roland Deah walked into my office.

I failed a literature class in college. At that time, I was unable to comprehend how to form a creative thought and then place it in logical pattern on paper. Naturally, I never considered tackling a book project. Roland Deah changed all that.

The experiences and lessons of my life are only included in this book through the encouragement and persistence of Ed Chinn. Ed saw the parallel tracks of God's dealing with Roland and with me – two very different men through vastly dissimilar life canvases – during our traumatic experiences. In addition, Ed's literary expertise has enabled the following presentation to take on a life that I was incapable of providing on my own.

Pastor Robert Furrow, Pastor of Calvary Chapel, Tucson, Arizona has had the greatest influence on my life. Every week, Robert tells and illustrates that God has a race for each of us to run. As soon as we accept Him into our lives and maintain a daily relationship with Him, God will reveal that race!

Ed Chinn

First, I thank our mutual friend Stan Moser for building a bridge for Ron Swager and I to meet.

Second, I will never forget July 8, 2011. At 10:00 a.m. on that day, Ron Swager, Roland Deah, and I met in the dusty little town of Florence, Arizona. Ducking out of the intense heat (it hit 118 later that day), we slipped into a private back room in a dark, and mercifully cool, restaurant. That is where I heard the story you are preparing to read. It took my breath away. More importantly, I met two men who felt like brothers then and do even more so today. I cherish them as friends; I look forward to whatever God may have in store for us beyond this book.

Many others have provided tremendous assistance as we compiled notes, did interviews, and wrote this book. We especially thank Denise Churchill, Pauline Mujawamariya, John Boaz, Mona Snelson, Paul Chinn,

Kelly Scherrer, Gary and Nancy Paetzold, Mike and Pam Bishop, Stephanie Cowart, Amy McArthy, and Pam Godwin.

We also thank Maggie Edgerton for her excellence as a proofreader and Karen Williams and Brecca Theele for their artistic brilliance in cover and interior design of this book.

PRELUDES

Ed Chinn

For two decades, Charles Taylor, warlord-turned-President of Liberia, launched tsunamis of terror across Liberia and Sierra Leone.

Under international pressure, he finally resigned from the Presidency in 2003. He was also indicted in 2003 and has been in UN custody since 2006. At last, on April 26, 2012, Taylor, one of the largest and most feared "elephants" of the forest, was convicted of eleven counts of crimes against humanity. On May 30, he was sentenced to fifty years in prison.

Every elephant has two days: the day of his frightening power and the day of his equally frightening judgment.

So many of history's terrorists are no longer remembered. Although they once brought epic dimensions of death and destruction, in the end they blew away like chaff in a windstorm. David wrote of this in Psalm 37:

> Yet a little while and the wicked man will be no more; And you will look carefully for his place, and he will not be there.

> But the humble will inherit the land, And will delight themselves in abundant prosperity.

> The wicked plots against the righteous, And gnashes at him with his teeth. The Lord laughs at him; For He sees his day is coming.

The story you are about to read takes place in a very dangerous time and place. But it is profoundly relevant to your life; the terrorists you face – whether physical, financial, relational, vocational, or other – will blow away. They are diseased and dying. None are immortal. Join in the higher view and laugh at them. Their day is coming.

Ed Chinn
November 1, 2012
Columbia, Tennessee

Ron Swager

I also once knew an elephant. Mine sat on my chest. That crushing, paralyzing, deadly weight is probably what sensitized me – fourteen years later – to Roland Deah's incredible story of surviving other elephants.

All of human history is a story of surviving terrible odds. People have always been pulverized under the feet of warring elephants. Roland's were African terrorists. Mine were more "civilized." Yours may take other forms. But they are all very real and very deadly.

I am a practical man. I tend to see things in pretty clear, even utilitarian, terms. I want to share two things that I know:

People always have options. There is something every person can do. People are never without a choice. There is no such thing as total defeat. There is never a disaster so devastating that a person cannot pull something out of the ashes.

God has given every human a race to run. I first heard that idea from Pastor Robert Furrow. We are not called to analyze, doubt, or talk things to death; we are called to run a race. In the immortal words of Nike, "Just do it."

Even though I did not hear that idea from Pastor Furrow until I was almost sixty, I have lived my life in a subconscious pursuit of it. I've always been a man of action. Like a shark, I have to keep moving. Knock me down; I will not stay there.

Then I met a young African man, Roland Deah, who was and is a stainless steel exemplar of that idea. Knocked down hard and often in his young life, he has always bounced back to the balls of his feet. At eight years old, he was clobbered by blows that would have landed larger and older men in hospitals or morgues.

His loved ones were shot and blown to pieces. As a small boy, he saw men hacked to death by machetes, women savagely raped, and endless rivers of refugees carrying nothing and walking toward the unknown.

Yet, he never quit. He had a race to run. To my everlasting gratitude, one day his race brought him through a waiting room in my company.

Every one of you reading this book knows the terrible and crushing blows that can knock you down. Perhaps the real message here is: you have a choice. Like a boxer on the canvas, you can lie there or you can get back up. Yes, it is that simple.

I hope you will get up. You have a race to run. I want to encourage and equip you to do that. If you still have questions after reading this book, find me. Let's go have coffee. Tell me your story. I'll be your friend. I want to help you get back in the race.

Ron Swager
November 1, 2012
Tucson, Arizona

I will make a covenant of peace with them and rid the land of savage beasts so that they may live in the wilderness and sleep in the forests in safety.

I will make them and the places surrounding my hill a blessing. I will send down showers in season; there will be showers of blessing. The trees will yield their fruit and the ground will yield its crops; the people will be secure in their land.

They will know that I am the Lord, when I break the bars of their yoke and rescue them from the hands of those who enslaved them.

They will no longer be plundered by the nations, nor will wild animals devour them. They will live in safety and no one will make them afraid.[1]

CHAPTER 1

JUST ANOTHER HOT DAY IN TUCSON

Slamming car doors and loud shouts awakened the little boy in his upstairs bedroom. A moment later, the front door disintegrated into splinters and dust from a barrage of machine gun fire. He sprang out of bed and rolled under it as a deep male voice announced, "Kill these Krahn dogs." More gunfire ripped the house and family.

The boy under the bed heard the screams of his dying Grand Mama and Uncle Walter. He could also hear his own heartbeat thumping loudly against the wood floor. They hear my heartbeat; I will die.

The boy left his childhood in that bloody room...

And then all was quiet as the stillness of death blanketed the house. The boy heard the door open as the killers announced they would find them at their business. They had missed their real targets, the boy's parents. In that moment, the boy knew he would soon be an orphan. These men would not stop until the family was dead and their wealth stolen.

He remained under the bed several excruciating hours until he knew the house was safe. Then he slowly climbed out from under the bed, crept down the stairs, and walked through the slaughterhouse; Grand Mama and Walter's bullet-riddled corpses lay in the blood-splattered living room. The stench of blood permeated the house.

The boy left his childhood in that bloody room as he ran to the safety of the forest.

I am sitting in the very plush waiting room of my company, gazing into the eyes of the young Liberian man telling me his astounding story. As tears flow down my face, I realize he might as well be from Mars; the distance between us could not be greater.

In addition to the stark contrast of our skin colors, I look back over a life that had been a very sweet ride. Great genes, excellent parents (to their only child), and a face-to-the-wind brashness that charmed many and pissed off a few. Most people considered me good looking, smart, and even fearless and daring; I always swung for the fences. I have managed to build some wealth.

For most of my life, I lived in a dazzling swirl of fine restaurants, beautiful women (I dated many and married some), gorgeous golf courses, and exotic lighting reflected in gin martinis and through laughter and the aromatic smoke of fine cigars.

Two hours ago I knew nothing about this man sitting in front of me. Yet, I feel a kinship with him. His story reverberates through the corridors of my heart. In this young man and his story, I have collided with part of my own destiny. I know I am changed because of this story and the man telling it.

Two hours ago, I only knew that May 27, 2011 was another hot day in Tucson. Nothing under the cloudless blue-white sky alerted me to a change as my black Yukon rolled to a stop in front of my office. Over the hood, I watched a gleaming white Mercedes sedan of golfers glide through the entrance to the Tucson Country Club. I wished I had time to join them. Shrugging off my disappointment, I stepped out of my SUV, walked through the front door and straight into my office. I did not notice the man in the waiting area.

After slowly reading the morning paper, I walked out into the waiting area. That's the first time I ever saw Roland Deah. He was sitting quietly, reading a Bible. Just over his head was a wall collage, containing a whisper of change: "Think of the possibilities."

For some reason not grasped at the time or now remembered, I sat down near him.

As we began to talk, I learned that he was in my Christian Companion Senior Care office to apply for a job. Roland had driven past our office, saw the sign, and decided to make an appointment to apply for part-time work. He had been looking for a job that would permit him to attend Pima Community College in the coming fall (2011) semester. Our Director, who had scheduled the interview, had been delayed.

Roland is a large and a young man. His black eyes are older and wiser, while his round cherubic face is younger and more playful, than his twenty-nine years. His hair and goatee are cut very short. His skin is as black as ivory is white.

As I listened to his musical voice, I could not identify his deep African accent. When I asked, Roland smiled.

"Liberia," he answered.

"What brought you to America?"

"The Civil War."

LIBERIA

Most Americans do not know anything about Liberia, even though it is one of the most pro-American countries in the world.

The Republic of Liberia is located on the southwest corner of western Africa, between Sierra Leone and Ivory Coast. Liberia has approximately three hundred and fifty miles of "ocean-front property" on the Atlantic. The country is about the size of Tennessee.

The nation of Liberia came into existence as a solution to a largely American problem. As slavery slipped toward its inevitable collapse, America needed to find a place where freed slaves could carve out new lives in freedom and equality.

Of course, as with any historical convulsion, the origins and motives were mixed. The abolitionists wanted to see the slaves find genuine freedom – freedom from oppression and ownership, and freedom to their own opportunities. But another perspective was anxiety about the growing number of free blacks in America. Within twenty years, from 1790 to 1810, the number of freed slaves in the colonies increased from about 59,000 to more than 180,000. That 300% increase brought understandable concern and social tumult.

The founding documents of The Society for the Colonization of Free People of Color of America clearly saw and instituted the Republic of Liberia as a refuge for freed American blacks.

Although the venture represented the grand and celebrated "birth of a nation," the area was already home to thousands of native people. In fact, the area (called, at that time, Pepper Coast or Grain Coast) had been inhabited since the 12th century, perhaps longer. Of course, those indigenous people resented the incursion of the United States into their land. The resentment gave birth to derogatory names for both groups. "The Country People" were the descendants of the natives. "Congo People" referred to those who came from America (many disembarked at the Congo River).

In 1847, the Republic of Liberia was born. The government of the country remained in the Americo-Liberian hands for more than one hundred and thirty years. The United States backed the Americo-Liberian "True Whig Party" throughout various conflicts and crises during those years.

However, in 1980, the long-simmering contention between the indigenous "country people" and the Americo-Liberian rulers finally exploded into a very bloody coup d' état against the government. President William R. Tolbert was assassinated on April 12, 1980. Ten days later, thirteen of his cabinet members were executed. The leader of the insurrection, Samuel K Doe, a member of the Krahn tribe, became the first non-Americo-Liberian President in Liberia's history.

President Doe did not – perhaps could not – lead Liberia into the promised peace, prosperity, and freedom. Instead, he established a military regime that smothered all opposition. However, he said the military regime would be temporary; civilian government would be restored. It never was.

In 1989, the American-educated Charles Taylor, a former Doe government official, formed the National Patriotic Front of Liberia. With the NPFL, he launched an insurrection against the Doe government on December 24, 1989. Nine months later, on September 9, 1990, Doe was captured and killed. As a warlord, Taylor controlled much of Liberia. But an internal power struggle produced a new force when Prince Johnson, a key Taylor supporter, broke away from the NPFL and formed the INPFL, the Independent National Patriotic Front of Liberia.

At that point, Liberia fell into a full-blown civil war. Both sides – Taylor's NPFL and Johnson's INPFL – committed horrendous acts of terror and barbarism. They roiled and destabilized the country with fire, rape, murder, and cannibalism. The warlords lived out the African proverb – "When the bull elephants fight, the grass always loses."

The civil war would result in the death of 250,000 people – 10% of the entire nation. It was also estimated that 70% of all Liberian women were raped during the war.

When the bull elephants fight, the grass always loses.

On September 12, 1990 (three days after the murder of President Doe), the civil war exploded into Zwedru, Liberia. The fury of that day fire balled right into a peace-loving family named Deah.

That is where Roland's story begins.

lthough the environment of Zwedru in the 1980s would have seemed primitive to children in the West – especially under clouds of national crises, like financial collapse, a severe military regime, and numerous attempted insurrections – Roland Deah enjoyed a fine childhood.

In the peaceful and slow rhythms of life in that time and place, the days seemed to last forever. Adults sat on chairs, porches, or on the ground and listened to the laughter and shouts of children chasing fireflies. The pulsing and glowing trails of light pulled squealing children back and forth across darkening yards and toward the forest.

Sundays were very unhurried, quiet, and peaceful days. People slept late. Roland remembers that, on Sunday "everything stopped. People relaxed." He also remembers the streets of Zwedru as still and quiet (as contrasted with the weekday hustle of automobile horns, bleating animals, and petroleum stench).

The Deah family attended services in a Catholic church (Liberia is a mostly Christian nation). The children also attended the best Christian schools. Roland's parents, Brown and Rebecca, taught the Christian faith to their children and prayed with them regularly and often. They taught and lived faith, trust, and gratitude.

In a city of huts, outdoor markets, and goats wandering along mud streets, the Deah family owned a sprawling five-bedroom white and yellow home. The concrete and brick house had electricity, three bathrooms, and a large back yard surrounded by walls of climbing bougainvillea and soothing shade trees. Another house with two bedrooms and a bathroom also occupied the property. Relatives often lived in that house.

Brown and Rebecca hosted many social gatherings on the vast and colorful grounds. The large front yard was, in fact, used by village children as a soccer field. Roland rode his three-wheeled cycle – two rear tires and one in the front – around and beyond the field.

Brown Deah was a wholesale merchant. He sold textiles, groceries, books, school supplies, and other life essentials. He was known in the city as a very successful businessman. In fact, at times, their large home served as a market. Roland remembers people filling the house to buy rice, tea, coffee, and other goods. The patterns of community naturally flowed to the Deah home.

Mr. Deah walked through Zwedru as a city elder. He was a tall man. His dress was regal; his gait conveyed royal deportment. Brown's soft and precise enunciation carried warmth and kindness to all who approached him. Even in his early thirties, he was known as a wealthy, wise and generous man.

His reputation was known further than they might have imagined. The warring "elephants" had also heard of this man.

A QUIET SUMMER MORNING

By late summer of 1990, Liberia had been churned by political turbulence for more than a decade. Just one year earlier, the nation had exploded into civil war. By September, a blanket of fear seemed to settle over Grand Gedeh County, heart of the Krahn territory, in southeastern Liberia. Many who lived in Zwedru, the capitol city of the Krahn people, had heard rumors of invasion for weeks. The noose was pulling tighter.

The rebel forces associated with Prince[2] Johnson, and his Independent National Patriotic Front of Liberia,

---

2 "Prince" is a common name for males in Liberia. It was not a title for Johnson.

targeted (among others) Krahn people. Partly because of the abuses by President Doe, resentment of Krahn people was very strong in Liberia. So, under Johnson's forces, Krahn people were in danger. Furthermore, the military had been so demolished that very little protection was available for the Krahn territory.

Just before 7:30 on a Wednesday morning, September 12, 1990, Brown and Rebecca Deah gathered two of their children – three-year-old Mona and the infant Patrick – and drove away in their green Datsun pickup. The drive to their place of business would take about ten minutes.

Their oldest child, eight-year-old Roland, remained at home with his grandmother ("grand mama"); two uncles, Walter and Paul; and Walter's son, Joe.[3]

In that moment, Roland knew he would soon be an orphan.

Moments after Brown and Rebecca drove away, Roland was awakened in his upstairs bedroom by the sound of slamming car doors and loud voices. Then he heard machine gun fire at their front door; the door was blown to pieces. Paul pulled Roland and Joe under the bed. The boys heard a man say, "Let's kill these Krahn dogs." More gunfire ripped the house and family. The

---

3 Four other Deah children – Brown, Angeline, Saysor, and Pacone – were out of town with relatives.

boys under the bed heard the screams of their dying family members.

And then it was quiet. The stillness of death. The murderers realized they had missed Brown and Rebecca. Roland heard them say they would find them at the business and left. In that moment, Roland knew he would soon be an orphan. These men would not stop until the Deah family was dead and their wealth stolen.

Simultaneous with the murderous assault on the Deah home, bombs exploded all over Zwedru. Machine guns and rockets turned the city into a bloody inferno of confusion, desperation, and death. Adults, children, and animals ran in terrified unison as bombs blew dirt high into the air and rockets screamed through houses and humans. Dead bodies and severed limbs littered the ground as people began running or stumbling down the road toward the Prime Timber Production Refugee Camp (PTP) outside of Zwedru. Hundreds of citizens started gathering at the camp. By nightfall, they would all be refugees.

Back at the Deah home, Roland, Joe, and their Uncle Paul remained under the bed "a few hours" until they knew the house was safe. Then they rolled out from under the bed, crept down the stairs, and walked through the slaughterhouse; Grand Mama and Walter lay dead in the blood-splattered living room. Joe screamed at the gruesome sight of his father's bullet-ridden body. The stench of blood permeated the house. Paul solemnly pushed his terrified and weeping nephews toward the door.

THE BOY IN RED

Paul Deah, uncle, protector and guide, tucked both his nephews under his arms and ran to the bushes at the edge of the forest. Many other Krahn villagers were screaming and running into the forest. Some were shot as they ran.

Soon, Paul and Roland and Joe were enveloped in the dense and presumably safe shrubs and undergrowth of the forest. But they could hear Taylor's soldiers in the near distance, rushing down the path toward them. The rebels began shooting in their direction. The greenery became a continuous blur as Paul tried throwing them off with hairpin turns. While skimming over fallen logs and ducking under branches, his ears trained on the bullets hissing by and ripping into nearby plants and trees. The soldiers were getting closer.

Then Cousin Joe's body fell slack in his arms as a 7.62-millimeter round tore through his flesh. Paul swerved off the path and slid down a steep bank, cleaving to the unconscious boy and to Roland. When they reached the bottom he laid his nephew in the grass and tried to revive him. As the gunfire subsided, he grabbed leaves to swab the massive bloody crater in the boy's back, but it was too late. Joe was already dead. Roland and Paul looked around; they had landed in a clearing. In the fleeting calm, Paul and Roland wondered if their pursuers had given up their chase. Maybe they had thrown the rebels off their track?

Then shouting in (indigenous phrase), "Down here!" The leader signaled the others.

Roland looked up the hillside just as the soldiers broke into the clearing. Suddenly, they were everywhere. Paul froze in disbelief as he stared at a mob of young children wielding AK-47s. He glanced back at his nephew's body. There was no time for grief, only blunt instinct. Survival was about to be measured in fractions of inches and seconds.

The rebels opened fire again.

He scooped Roland up into his great long arms and flew through knee-high grass, weaving and dodging another furious storm of bullets, eyes locked on the wall of foliage ahead. Breathless and running like a gazelle, Paul hurtled through brush, dropped down slides, bounded up hills, and ran into a green oblivion.

By outrageous fate, Roland wore his school uniform – red pants and shirt. Because the rebels wore red clothing, the little boy became instantly identified as a child soldier.

Child soldier?

In one of the more perverse realities of the Liberian civil wars, all sides recruited as many as 20,000 children as soldiers. With some as young as three years old, the children were terrorized, sleep-deprived, and drugged into committing inexplicable acts of terror. According to testimony before the Liberia Truth and Reconciliation Commission and other official committees, they raped, murdered, beheaded, and cannibalized their fellow Liberians – adults and children.

Because the children were so dehumanized, they became monsters. "Jefferson," a child soldier, told the Straight From the Heart radio audience that when he was seven years old, "…my commander and one of his deputies started arguing. They made a bet about a pregnant woman… The rebel leader said the woman had a boy child in her stomach. His deputy said she had a girl child. They bet two hundred U.S. dollars.

"Then my commander called me over. He said, 'Jefferson!' I said, 'Sir chief?' He say, 'Open that woman! I want to see which child is in her stomach!' She was screaming. Crying 'Lord, Lord. Lord.' I opened that woman raw to see what sex she was having. And the child was a male child, so my commander was happy.

He got two hundred dollars U. S. for his trouble. And the woman died. And her baby died."[4]

One boy told of the rebels chopping his brother "into little pieces before my eyes"[5] as a recruitment tool.

The psychological impact was horrendous; one observer spoke of old men's faces on children's bodies.

Former President Jimmy Carter, who served as an emissary for the U.S. to Liberia during the civil war, explained part of the matrix that pushed warlords to conscript children as soldiers: "Technological developments in weaponry, especially small arms, have made semiautomatic rifles light enough to be used, and simple enough to be stripped and reassembled, by a 10-year-old child."[6]

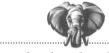

The bridge back to his life was completely and irreparably demolished.

So, in an ironic double danger, eight-year-old Roland, dressed in red, became a target of government

4 Agnes Fallah Kamara-Umunna and Emily Holland, *And Still Peace Did Not Come* (New York, NY: Hyperion Books, 2011) p. 2

5 Ibid., p. 145

6 Jimmy Carter, "Kid Soldiers a War's Most Tragic Victims," *USA Today*, June 30, 1998, copyright © 2011, The Carter Center troops as well as, almost certainly, an objective for deployment by the rebels. How would a little boy survive on that perilous high wire?

One day – September 12, 1990 – became the continental divide of Roland Deah's life. He had awakened in a fine home, comfortable bed, and the privileges brought by family wealth. But, as the day ended, he faced the same need for food, clothing, and shelter that the most primitive humans on the planet faced eons ago.

In one day, Roland lost his parents, brothers, sisters, grandmother, uncle, cousin, home, and his childhood. Furthermore, the bridge back to his life was completely and irreparably demolished.

CHAPTER 3

RUNNING FOR LIFE

The next morning, Roland awoke in the forest, next to his Uncle Paul on a mattress of leaves. He was hungry and scared. Those conditions would describe almost every day for the next two years.

What does a child do, living in the forests of Africa?

Alongside Paul and Roland were many other adults traveling with their children. The throng of evacuees became a rootless village, always on the move and seeking protection from enemies on every side. Because they were nomadic, school activities ceased. Most children had to go without familiar toys and other playthings that might have distracted them from all the pain and suffering. But there were other simple distractions that helped pass the time. The kids often gathered in the mornings to play soccer. Children used their shared abilities to improvise; rocks and sticks became goalposts and markers. Add a ball to kick around and that was all they needed for hours of entertainment.

Sometimes they would go down to a little creek in the hot afternoons to swim and bathe. If they had a group of at least ten kids, they'd split into two groups and play lengthy games of hide-and-seek in the edges of the forest, but always where it was safe and under watchful eyes of the adults. They played like this for long periods of time until the adults called them to go eat. After dinner they went out to play again until dark. Then it was time for bed.

In the evenings, the adults sat around and discussed politics. They talked about the war and mainly about Charles Taylor. Roland remembers that the infamous rebel was almost always the topic of discussion. "Soldiers cut out a child's heart and brought it to Taylor for his dinner." "Charles Taylor sealed the doors of a church last Sunday and burned everyone alive."

People moved to and from the makeshift village every day. Roland remembers waking up every morning not knowing which of his friends had moved on in the night. Companions would vanish without notice. Roland had no way to contact them. Some people would dwell among them for weeks or months and then they'd be gone the next day. New travelers would arrive to fill the empty space.

Roland's best friend, Boniface Chia, was like a brother. They spent their days playing soccer and hide-and-seek and splashing in the cool waters of the creek together. They slept next to each other every night on the same tank. Roland had found a renewed joy in the Chia family circle and called Boniface's mom and dad "auntie" and "uncle."

They shared devotions every morning while the women prepared the food. Uncle Paul would go into the forest and cut down plantains or gather cassava plants to contribute. If they were lucky enough to camp near a mango tree, they would have the young boys shimmy up the tree and shake down some fresh mangos for breakfast.

They always began each day with a prayer for the war to stop, their children to go back to school, and that people who lost family members would find them. Scripture verses were quoted from memory because nobody had a Bible. They clapped their hands and sang songs but in low hushed tones. They didn't want to draw adverse attention to themselves.

Roland showed up for devotions one morning, but Boniface did not join them. Roland discerned a different mood in the camp. None of the other kids were there either, not even Boniface's little sisters. Something must be very wrong.

Then, as Roland remembers, "People were crying and I didn't know why. Boniface's dad came and told me that my best friend had died in the middle of the night.

He died in his sleep right next to me and I didn't even know it."

The grief-stricken adults wept as they ushered Roland away. He stayed with the other kids to grieve, alone and uncomforted, while Boniface's father and a few men went to bury his best friend in the forest.

"Oh, it was cholera that killed him," everyone lamented. Roland didn't even know he was sick. Instead of a proper funeral, they cried for two or three days. Roland felt a deep hurt and loneliness after losing such a close companion.

Because he was just a child, intensely focused on survival, Roland does not know exactly how long he lived in the forest. But, based on available information, date construction, and memory, two years is the best guess. In that time, they only covered about one hundred meandering miles. At times, they camped for long periods with other refugees.

As Roland and Paul slowly and carefully navigated southeast toward Ivory Coast, they wore the only clothes they owned and slept on the ground. Paul hunted or trapped deer, monkeys, and other animals for food. Uncle and nephew scraped the forest floor to gather leaves, snails, grub worms, insects, and other "edibles."

They scooped their water from rivers. Of course, they had to remain alert in order to survive venomous snakes, scorpions, and poisonous insects.

Deadly snakes are common in sub-Saharan Africa. Paul and Roland cautiously shared the same routes with cobras, arboreal green mambas, black mambas, western bush vipers, and puff adders, all well-cloaked in their natural habitat and ready to strike at any perceived threat. When on their turf, avoiding them was nearly impossible.

Roland had learned in school that the fastest land snake in the world is the aggressive black mamba. It had a reputation of being the most respected and feared snake in all of Africa. In short bursts they can top speeds of ten to twelve miles per hour over level ground; if Paul or Roland happened to startle or anger one, outrunning it would not have been an option! This intimidating snake can grow up to 14 feet and races along with its head held up to four feet off the ground – about eye level for a boy like Roland. It would have been more merciful to be taken instantly by a rebel's bullet than suffer a slow, agonizing death from a venomous snake like the black mamba.

So many people had been displaced by the turbulence of the civil war that fleeting communities of refugees formed in the forest. Naturally, the transient communities became information networks for finding food. Word spread on where they could find cassava plants, plantains, or abandoned farms, offering rice, palm, cabbage, and other produce. Some refugees carried and shared cooking implements, pots, and pans.

Someone in the camp heard a soldier mutter that they would return the next day to kill the boy.

Troops – part of the provisional "United Liberation Movement of Liberia for Democracy (ULM) – often invaded the provisional camps of refugees and confiscated food supplies and utensils; they had to eat too. But the government troops, supposedly the good guys, represented a more severe threat for Roland. Because of his red clothing, the troops were certain that he was a child soldier.

One day, the ULM troops stormed the camp in search of supplies. One of them spotted a young boy wearing the red uniform of Taylor's rebels. He seized Roland.

"You are one of Taylor's killers!" he shouted. He began tying his hands so they could execute him. Paul screamed and pleaded for them to leave the boy alone.

"No!" cried Paul. "You will kill an innocent child!"

A soldier shouted, "Why do you protect a rebel? He is wearing red, just like the NPLF!"

"He is wearing his school uniform! He is a schoolboy who has done no wrong. Leave him alone!" Paul would not give up.

To silence the very determined and wildly emotional Paul, they shoved a terrified Roland to the ground and left. But someone in the camp heard a soldier mutter that they would return the next day to kill the boy.

Paul, the always-vigilant protector of his nephew, knew they must leave that location immediately. But doing so would only stir the hornet's nest. The boy in red was an easy target and the angry squad would not be satisfied until they tracked him down like an animal and carried out their threats of violence. One man overheard the troop's plan to return and execute Roland. He called Paul to the side and offered a way of escape.

"I have a large mattress," he whispered. "We can hide the boy inside it and smuggle him out of the camp." By intervening, this man had risked his own well being to save Roland, a stranger.

Such alliances were often forged between countrymen fighting a common enemy. The old idea of "strength in numbers" gained new significance during the war and was well practiced by those desperate to survive. Certainly, this kind of wisdom is never more accepted than when it can save your life.

With the help of other forest people, Paul and the

man rolled Roland into the old, queen-size mattress and tied it securely. The three of them left that night and (over a period of several months) carried the boy all the way to the Cavalla River.

CROSSING THE CAVALLA

Refugees represent one of the tragic themes in human history. Through the force of fire, disease, war, famine, or economic collapse, they often lose everything in an instant. The only choices available to them are sometimes as bad as what they are escaping. It is precisely the same raging predicament that many people faced in the horrendous heat of the World Trade Center on September 11, 2001. The "refugees," fleeing the burning towers, had no choice but to seek the sweet freedom of the cool air. In so doing, they fell to their deaths.

For many fleeing Liberians in 1990, Ivory Coast – a West African economic power and peaceful country – became the best choice as a refuge. So, crossing the Cavalla River, which forms more than half of the border, became a grand goal. But for many, including Roland Deah, death followed them across the Cavalla.

Wide as the Mississippi in places, the swift water of the Cavalla River carries many dangers. Hippos kill more people than any other animal in Africa. Crocodiles come in at a close second. The Cavalla is home to both of these hungry and hostile creatures.

When Paul and Roland arrived at the edges of the river, there were no large, modern ferries there to carry them to safer lands. Instead, a primitive means of transport moved at a sluggish pace. The river became a choke point where thousands of refugees waited to cross in dugout canoes that carried only two or three people at a time. (And at least one person had to bring the boat back across the river to pick up more passengers.) Like

Men, women, and children, plunged like herded cattle into the churning river, only to drown or be eaten alive.

the Israelites waiting to cross the river Jordan into the Promised Land, Roland remembers the cruelness of that prolonged delay. The land of "milk and honey" was within eyesight. But death prowled these shores daily. Periodic raids would send a panic through the crowds that were pinned along the brim of the water. To escape the gunfire, men, women, and children, plunged like herded cattle into the churning river, only to drown or be eaten alive.

Finally, the day arrived for them to journey into a new land. Would they find peace for their weary souls? When they shoved off from the beachhead, Roland charted the area in search of large dark stones floating on the water's surface – hippos. They are fiercely territorial. An irate hippopotamus could easily flip a canoe like the one he was in. As they paddled the tiny vessel across the wide, perilous waters to the other side, they thanked God for bringing them safely thus far. Maybe they would survive after all?

Roland believes that he and his Uncle Paul crossed the Cavalla sometime in 1992. They were among two hundred thousand Liberians seeking refuge in Ivory Coast.

They settled in the relative peaceful setting of Tai. These wandering exiles lived in one room, but it was far more safe and comfortable than living on the ground. To earn money, Paul did contract work with one of the local cocoa farms. He also went fishing and sold the fish in the village. Compared to their high standard of living before the war, their existence now was squalid and pitiable. But they considered this a safe and prosperous time when measured against their grim flight in through wilderness.

Paul continued his unrelenting protection of Roland. He enrolled the boy in a French school and made sure he had food and clothing. Roland remembers that his uncle kept him by his side. They lived in peace.

But three years later, on June 13, 1995, other Liberian men crossed the Cavalla. Their incursion brought savage death to the Tai region. The specific issue was a gold and diamond deal gone bad. Liberian rebels, trafficking gold and diamonds, murdered police officers, immigration officials and other government representatives, mob-style, in retaliation for failure to pay.

Then, in a reaction far too common to Africa, Ivory Coast residents ("Ivoirians") started killing Liberians. At that point, at least two hundred thousand Liberians lived as refugees in Ivory Coast. Perhaps, in a collective paroxysm, the Ivorians felt the need to purge themselves of the very essence of Liberia in their midst. Or, maybe it was a convenient excuse to push back on the crush of Liberian migration.

When Elephants Fight

Whatever the specific emotions and motives, the larger context for the murders and retaliation was Africa's long and tragic history of violence. The cycles of ferocity across the recent history of the African continent is traceable, in part, to colonialism.

For many reasons – mainly economic, racial, and religious – Europe began carving up Africa in the late 19th century. By 1914, virtually the entire continent was controlled by France, England, Italy, Portugal, and other nations. Beginning in the 1950s, Africans began fighting back against imperialism. Not only did they move in brutal confidence about the whole idea of liberation, but in doing so, they sanctioned violence as a means of solving twentieth century disputes. That led to several decades of civil wars throughout Africa.

Civil wars are, for many reasons, always messy. One of the most hideous characteristics of civil war is that civilians bear the crushing load of death; the wars are fought in their fields, factories, and front yards. Safe zones disappear. Humanitarian efforts – like the Red Cross or UN relief agencies – vanish because the workers cannot be protected. So death and other human disasters quickly proliferate across the land.

And, of course, wars must be financed. So natural resources get sucked into the machinery of war. In Africa, that means diamonds and gold.

That's why Africans know more deeply than anyone else that "When the elephants fight, the grass always loses." For most of the twentieth century, the bull elephants – the warlords, the rebels, and the "liberators" – have pulverized the "grass" of Africa. Millions have died because of the continuous cycles of violence on the continent.

On that day, June 13, 1995, the day the Liberian rebels murdered Ivorian officials and the Ivorians retaliated, the trampling elephants brought death closer to Roland. Sitting in his classroom at school, he heard the shooting. It brought an instant flashback to the day he lost his family in Zwedru. The nightmare was about to roll over him again. He knew he had to get to Uncle Paul. So he jumped up and ran out of his classroom and out of the school.

Running as fast as he could toward his and Paul's one-room home, he was suddenly overwhelmed by a surge of people running toward him. Everyone seemed to be fleeing Tai. Like a cork in a river, Roland was picked up by the flood of people and carried further away from home.

Amidst the stampede of people, Roland saw a neighbor lady. "What is happening," he screamed. She told him the Ivory Coast people were killing Liberian men. She said, "Young and old, they kill them."

"I saw it. They tied and blindfolded him. Then, they shot him to death."

Then, she added, "I'm sorry to tell you that they shot Paul. I saw it. They tied and blindfolded him. Then, they shot him to death."

For 13-year-old Roland, the lights went out.

For the second time in five years, the roaring and rampaging bull elephants destroyed his safe place.

They killed the only person he had left, the kind and protective Uncle Paul. Once again, Roland was a refugee, fleeing another jungle war. Once again, he faced the most desperate and most primitive needs – food, clothing and shelter. But this time he had no adult to shoulder the burden. He would never again see the room that had been "home" for three years.

CHAPTER 4

THE TERRORS OF DEATH

Thousands of Liberians fled from Tai to avoid the slaughter. Like other exiles in history, they formed a human river, gorging the dusty roads leading away from death. Rolled along like a pebble by that human river was one grieving and terrified 13-year-old boy. Roland was more alone than he had ever been before.

Today, he remembers that he walked and prayed. All that Brown and Rebecca Deah had cultivated in their children – prayer, faith, trust and gratitude – sprouted in Roland's heart. Although he does not remember what he prayed, he knows that his heart's cry must have mirrored David's anguish and supplication centuries earlier:

> Give ear to my prayer, O God,
> And do not hide Yourself from my supplication.
> Attend to me, and hear me…

Because of the voice of the enemy,

Because of the oppression of the wicked;

For they bring down trouble upon me,

And in wrath they hate me.

My heart is severely pained within me,

And the terrors of death have fallen upon me.

Fearfulness and trembling have come upon me,

And horror has overwhelmed me.[7]

Amidst thousands of his Liberian brothers and sisters, Roland walked to the city of Guiglo, about one hundred miles away. But death followed them. Incredibly, the highest levels of the Ivory Coast government had issued permission for Ivorians to kill any Liberian male older than ten.

Roland remembers, "Many people died on the road to Guiglo." All along the tragic migration, Ivorian citizens would come out of nowhere to attack the refugees with guns and machetes. They literally hacked and shot males, including children, to death. Although women were exempted from the killing, many were raped or stolen.

At thirteen, Roland could be legally killed. Amazingly, his school uniform saved his life. Five years earlier, his school uniform – red shirt and pants – had marked him for death by troops because red

---

7 Psalm 55: 1- 5, Scripture taken from the New King James Version. Copyright © 1982 by Thomas Nelson, Inc. Used by permission. All rights reserved.

was the rebel color. But, on the road to Guiglo, a new fate found him dressed in his French school uniform. Additionally, he spoke very fluent French. So when death approached, his "French citizenship" saved his life. Numerous times.

A Place Called Peace

When the thousands of Liberian refugees arrived in Guiglo, they had no place to go. No refugee camp had been established. So the United Nations quickly organized a food distribution point at a very large warehouse. As others arrived, the warehouse became a makeshift camp for the rising tide of displaced humanity.

The rapidly growing village of tents, warehouses, and mud just kept pushing the forests back. Because of sanitation problems, disease quickly spread through the population. Measles, chicken pox, malaria, cholera, and other illnesses began claiming lives. Every morning, a cart gathered up those who had died during the night.

The camp eventually became "Peace Town," the shamefully titled refugee camp. The camp provided no peace, no security or protection at all (although the United Nations did try to maintain some level of safety). Women were raped daily. And, the killing of Liberian males continued. Every night, military personnel came to the camp, took males away and executed them.

However, once again, a kind and protective adult came into Roland's life. The neighbor lady who had witnessed Paul Deah's death became Roland's protector and "mother." She cooked meals and made sure he was always nourished as well as possible.

Roland remembers the small gatherings by the evening fire. The singing in a unified, hypnotic sway to the music. Weeping and shouting. The constant thrum of crickets in his ears. One night, the neighbors, who had butchered a goat earlier that day, brought several skewers of cooked meat and rice bread to share. For Roland, the slaughtered goat carcass aroused a vision of a blood-saturated room. Brutal massacre…bodies…loss. The thought had Roland's eyes welling with tears, but he held them in check. A plume of smoke whirled up and stung his eyes. He stepped away and let the tears fall freely.

In the glow of the fire, a lost child cried for her mamma. People looked on with indifference. It made him feel like he was the only one in the world who understood her. They were both lost. But he would never again be "found" the way he wanted to.

Roland approached the child and offered his bread to her. She reached out and clutched it in her tiny hand. After a fit of hushed sobs, she bit into it.

"Sabina!" A mother rushed in to pick her up.

"Mamma!"

The bread dropped from her hand into the fire.

Roland took a deep, heavy breath as he watched the rice bread turn black in the hot flames.

"Yes, it does seem that we have someone named Deah, a thirteen-year-old boy named Roland."

The humidity hung like an oppressive millstone around him.

Oh, how he wanted to be found!

A MAN OF PEACE

Henri Paulet, a Krahn and a French professor at the University of Cocody in Abidjan, Ivory Coast, had been a friend of Brown Deah's since the 1980s.

Knowing well the political turmoil in Liberia, Professor Paulet became concerned about his friend. When he could not reach him, he exhausted every means of research in trying to find some news of Brown or his family. He found nothing.

After five years of dead ends, the father of four drove seven hours to the Peace Town camp. Searching for anyone named Deah, Professor Paulet spent three days at the refugee camp. He walked through the dusty sea of heartbreak – wails of desperation and grief, sick and dying and dead people, barking dogs, naked and malnourished children, UN logos, and the stench of feces.

Finally, he had a breakthrough. A registrar of refugees listened to the Christian gentleman's story of trying to find a friend. Yes, it does seem that we have someone named Deah, a thirteen-year-old boy named Roland.

Hours later, Paulet gazed at the son of Brown Deah. He saw a despondent and fearful boy. The wise friend reached out slowly; his voice and his hands were gentle. African definitions of family are often elastic, and the professor wanted to build trust and common ground. So, he told Roland, "I am your uncle, but you can call me Dad."

Roland's fear slipped. Surely, here was a trustworthy and stable man. He agreed to go with the professor. So, after one year in the very dangerous place called "Peace," Roland climbed into Paulet's white Range Rover and left that place forever. The seven-hour drive to Abidjan took Roland beyond the reach of deprivations and government-sanctioned murder.

Through the kindness of Henri Paulet, the orphaned Roland stepped into a timeless pattern wherein God proves Himself to be "a father for the fatherless…He makes a home for the lonely." (Psalm 68: 5 – 6). Roland found a home with Henri and Juliet Paulet and their four children in Abidjan. After six years of uncertainty, hunger, peril, and lost childhood, the Paulets and their large four-bedroom home became Roland's safe place. It was almost too good to be true.

Henri and Juliet formally adopted Roland. After six years, the young teenager was once again part of a family. His prayers shifted from entreaty to gratitude. He lived a normal life of family, school, church, and peaceful pursuits.

CHAPTER 5

OTHER ELEPHANTS

Roland's story tore me out of Tucson and dropped me far away, in a completely alien time and place. I did not know how long I had been listening to this heartbreaking and captivating saga. But the tyranny of my own bodily needs finally pulled me back to my own life on a hot day in Tucson. I had to take a break.

As I washed and dried my hands in my office lavatory, I thought about the crushing load borne by such a young man. Orphaned, terrorized, and forced beyond the safety of childhood. What is that hideous darkness that roars out of a clear day to wound, cripple, or kill?

Although Roland lived in what we would call a primitive, or third-world nation, for the first seven years of life he knew the tranquility of safety, peace and prosperity. His family had built proper insulation for their children. They protected them from the terrors of the jungle. They did all they could. Nothing else could be expected of them. And yet, in one hour, it all vanished.

How was that any different from the profound safety surrounding the most powerful man in the world, the President of the United States? Yet, a single bullet exploded the illusion of protection and instantly destroyed President John Kennedy a few years ago.

Is anyone really safe? What does safety mean?

Different jungles breed different elephants. Although I could never compare my ordeal to Roland's, I remembered the summer of my fiftieth year. In 1997 – just as Roland was settling into a new life of relative safety with the Paulet family – a different elephant trampled my life.

I had just returned from two weeks of golfing all the British Open courses in Scotland. On Saturday, June 21st, after a round of golf, sitting in the very posh Tucson Country Club, playing gin rummy with my regular group, I suddenly began feeling horrible.

"I don't feel well; I'm going home," I announced to my buddies. As I rolled out the gate, I began to feel worse. Much worse. Instead of going home, and because I had never felt like that before, I drove straight to Tucson Medical Center, just a little over a mile away.

I shot into the Med Center parking lot, slammed on the brakes, and rushed through the automatic sliding doors to the ER. As soon as I began describing my symptoms, nurses pulled me into the nearest triage room.

"Mr. Swager, what you're experiencing is called angina." My triage nurse, Becky, was very somber.

"What the heck is angina? And don't sugarcoat it." I didn't want the watered-down version. She obliged.

"It means you're a prime candidate for a full-blown heart attack."

I shook my head as if throwing off a curse she'd just placed on me. She wrapped a yellow elastic band around my bicep and cinched it tight, cutting off the circulation to my lower arm.

"A…uh…heart attack?" Hearing those words come out of my own mouth unnerved me.

"Yes, sir." Becky nodded as she thumped around, waiting for a fat vein to bulge to the surface.

"But I've always eaten healthy… Worked out all my life…" I said as though my words were so compelling that they would change the channel.

Becky didn't respond.

I've since learned that heart attacks have no regard for rebuttals. I drew a deep breath and released it very slowly.

"How bad off am I?"

"Depends." She poked the syringe into my flesh and

hit a gusher. The plump, juicy vein started flowing like an oil well, filling vial after vial with blood. After six, I stopped counting. It looked like I could have filled a blood bank. "We'll know more after your EKG."

Just then, a guy showed up at the door with a wheelchair. He hauled me to a room where they do the electrocardiograms. After my EKG, Dr. Santiago Ramirez came in to discuss the results.

"We didn't find anything significant on your EKG," Ramirez said.

I let out an audible sigh; relieved it might just be a false alarm. "I'm actually feeling pretty good right now, Doc."

He nodded. "That's good. But we're still a little concerned because your extremities are very cool. When was the last time you had a stress test?"

"Oh, at least ten years."

He shot me a look like a disapproving teacher about to make me stay in for recess. "That's too long. I'm going to order one for you." He scribbled some notes in my file.

"Great, I'll come in on Monday and get it done."

"Slow down, cowboy; let's do it tomorrow."

"OK, I'll be back first thing in the morning."

"Why don't you stay overnight as a precaution?"

That got my attention. "Okay, I live alone. No sense in pushing my luck," I said nonchalantly. But a warning buzzer was blaring in my brain.

Throughout that night, they woke me up every hour to extract more blood samples and to check my vitals. Thankfully, all the nurses were professional, courteous, and calming (and some were really good looking). The next morning, they wheeled me down the hall to take the stress test. On the way I started feeling just as I had while playing cards the afternoon before.

"It's back; I'm feeling the same way I did yesterday." My voice seemed unsteady.

The attendant immediately whisked me into the stress test room. She pulled me onto a table, quickly shaved my chest and slapped wires all over my nearly naked body. I looked down at the disturbing wires protruding from everywhere. Like Frankenstein's monster, it looked like I too was the subject of some mad science experiment gone awry. The only thing missing was the bolt of lightning. But then…as if on cue… Zwaap!! Out of nowhere a form of lightning struck.

The nurse suddenly ran across the room and started

punching numbers into the telephone. I heard the anxiety in her voice.

When she returned, I stammered, "You-you sound kind-kinda concerned."

"I'm getting a different reading than we had last night."

"Don't get excited. You're having a heart attack."

Ten seconds later an army of ER doctors and nurses burst into the room with equipment (that I later learned is known as a "crash kit"). They threw the crash kit on the floor and checked my blood pressure. Like war-zone medics, they stabbed an IV tube into my arm.

Dr. Ramirez strode into the room. "Are you okay?"

"Hell, no! Does this scene look like I'm okay?

The doctor studied me with practiced calm. It didn't take rocket science to read his body language. He was serious as a—

"Can someone please tell me what's going on?"

"Don't get excited," he said with a dead monotone. "You're having a heart attack." My arms and legs turned to rubber. The doctor hustled the team into a rapid response; they injected a fast acting sedative into the IV tube. The lights went out instantly.

Someone said that death is God's way of telling us to slow down. A heart attack gives a clear preview of that. When an elephant sits on your chest, you realize that all you ever were, all you ever felt, and all you ever believed does not matter. Even though you did not die in a final sense, you crossed over from one life to a new one. Nothing will ever be the same again.

Maybe I'm beginning to understand a little of what Roland experienced. I opened the door to go back to the waiting room to join my new friend.

OUT OF AFRICA

S ix years after Roland arrived in Abidjan, civil war broke out in Ivory Coast. Roland heard gunfire the night of September 19, 2002, when rebels tried to overthrow the government.

It seemed that an old story was starting to be told again.

In the very familiar saga of Western Africa, clouds of war rolled in over Ivory Coast. In early 2003, the United Nations saw a looming humanitarian crisis. So, with the Bush Administration, the UN created a resettlement program, allowing Ivory Coast citizens to seek refuge in America. With counsel from his adopted family, Roland applied for the program. On December 1, 2003, Roland told his story to UN officials in Abidjan. On December 19, he was approved for relocation to the United States.

Five days later, on Christmas Eve, Roland turned twenty-two. That would be his last birthday in his native

Africa. He learned that his destination would be Tucson, Arizona. When he Googled this new place, he discovered it to be on fire. Literally. Fires burned the mountains around Tucson; smoke choked the city. Although life was, once again, growing dangerous for Roland in Africa, he wondered if he would be traveling to a greater danger. After all, that had been a recurring pattern for several years.

Leaving the Paulet family and his native Africa was profoundly painful to him. He had lived in the Paulet house and name as long as he had lived as a Deah in Zwedru. This was his home. His head understood the life-changing advantage of moving to America. But his heart was ripped by the reality of leaving his lifelong identity with Africa, with Liberia. And leaving his dearly loved Paulet family broke his heart.

On February 4, 2004, Roland boarded an airplane for the first time in his life, one that would take him out of Africa. He left every familiar relationship, sight, sound, and sensibility. He was traveling deeper into the unknown.

Two days later, after plane changes in Paris, Atlanta, and Dallas, Roland walked up the jet way at Tucson International Airport. He knew that the Jewish Family and Children's Services of Tucson sponsored his "resettlement," but he did not know if anyone would actually meet him.

All the other passengers from his flight claimed their bags and left. Would anyone ever come for Roland?

Waiting was a familiar exercise for a boy who had been a refugee most of his life. He and his Uncle Paul had waited hours for killers to leave his home or for soldiers or rebels to pass by. Roland had waited for days for a cup of water or a bag of rice. He knew how to wait.

So he waited in the passenger pickup area of the airport, sitting on a bag that bore his name in large block letters. All the other passengers from his flight claimed their bags and left. Would anyone ever come for Roland? In a post-911 world, how long before airport personnel would become suspicious? Would he be arrested and jailed? After his long and emotional journey, perhaps he would be deported.

"Are you Roland Deah?"

He looked up into the lovely face of a young Russian woman named Semolina. Her soft beauty and kind eyes made him feel like she understood him. Later he learned that she too was a refugee. Of course, common experiences build bridges.

Semolina helped him load his bags and drove him to the Jewish Family and Children's Services office. The drive to the office took them through a bad part of town. What Roland saw from the car window – broken and boarded up windows, graffiti, hollow-eyed and menacing young men – clashed with all the reports and images of America. Roland told me that he "expected America to be the Garden of Eden. That was the way we saw America from Africa." Suddenly, his confusion boiled over; he turned to Semolina and asked, "Is this America?" She assured him that it was.

The New Land

Roland was quickly, efficiently and kindly "processed." The Jewish Family and Children's Services representative for Roland, Pauline Mujawamariya, was sensitive and very experienced with refugees. Because she too was a refugee (from Rwanda), she could easily see his anxiety, fears, turmoil, and blind spots.

Pauline took care of all his food, clothing, health, and housing needs. And she also helped him obtain a social security number and his own apartment. She and others who assisted him had no idea of the horrors he had seen or where he had walked in life, but they saw a distinct grace on the young man from Liberia. He was obviously educated, but he was also humble and considerate toward everyone, especially women. He laughed easily.

People were drawn to Roland; they wanted to help him. And, in fact, he needed help. He was struggling to adjust to this new land. For example, when he received his first paycheck, he walked into the bank to cash it. When the teller counted out several hundred dollars, Roland panicked: "No. Stop. Too much. It's only one hundred, twenty dollars!"

She smiled and continued to pile large bills on the counter.

"No. No. No. Stop!" He waved his hands and began backing out of the bank. He was afraid he would be arrested for bank robbery, so he ran all the way to Pauline. She returned to the bank with him. She and the teller explained that it really was twelve hundred dollars and it really was his money.

Shortly after that, Roland saw a car he liked on a used car lot. Seeing "$3,000" written across the windshield, he walked in to the office and announced he had come to buy that car. He would pay cash. When the eager salesman drew up the sales order, Roland counted out three hundred dollars and smiled. He was chased from the dealership (he did return later – when he had saved more money – and bought the very same car).

As a young black man in America, he heard frequent racial insults. And some Americans, hearing his accent, suggested that he "go back to Africa!" Roland could not understand; Liberia is very pro-American. As a small child, he had learned to love America. Yet, in America, he was often treated harshly. Furthermore, he had not met one American who knew anything about Liberia, let alone the civil wars. How could Americans be so ignorant of a nation that so deeply loved the United States?

Roland could not grasp how the U. S. news media could ignore the death of two hundred and fifty thousand people. How could less significant news items – like Washington, DC Mayor Marion Barry being busted for cocaine possession, Madonna's latest stage antics, or O. J. Simpson's trial – completely crowd out the horrors of a civil war?

He felt like he couldn't breathe; he had to talk to Henri Paulet. Pauline used her own cell phone to make the call.

When Henri heard his "son," he immediately discerned his troubled heart. Pauline saw how Roland's spirit calmed as he listened to his faraway adoptive father. Henri advised Roland to be careful, respectful, and honest. That was all he needed; the gentle voice, the wise words, the imparted confidence.

A few days later, Roland applied for a job as housekeeper at Tucson's elegant resort, Canyon Ranch. Located in the foothills of the Catalina Mountains, the magnificent spa has catered to the richest and most famous since the 1970s.

Roland, a Liberian refugee who had seen the most horrendous murders and violent rapes in front of his childhood eyes, walked through the extreme opposite of his long matrix of dispossession and terror – splendid stone and wood architecture, muted southwest décor, and lavish spreads of gourmet foods. He saw very wealthy people strolling across luxuriant, sculpted lawns on stone walkways. Beautiful and fragrant flowers scented the atmosphere.

As he passed near the front desk on his way to the office, Roland heard two couples struggling to communicate in French. Because he could hear the rising volume of problems, he stepped in. "May I help," he asked in French. The couples found fast rapport and comfort with the young black man. When he quickly solved their problem, the general manager suddenly appeared and hired Roland, on the spot, as a bellman!

Roland worked for Canyon Ranch all of two days

until the Tucson Unified School District (TUSD) called. They wanted an African to help their growing population of African students. So Roland moved on up from bellman into an educational career. He worked for TUSD for three and a half years.

For this gifted immigrant, the new land of America seemed to be a roller coaster of scary plunges and then soaring accolades and promotions. But he had survived the unimaginable through endurance and continually pushing his vulnerable heart up before His God. He knew he would make it. Somehow.

BRINGING THEM BACK

The old African proverb about fighting elephants and dying grass is, in fact, a tragic and true lyric about life in Africa. And, yes, it is a pattern of life on earth. The powerful and the ruthless have trampled, killed, and scattered the poor and the helpless for thousands of years.

No one knew that better than Roland Deah. Brutal warlords had

Brutal warlords had trampled, killed, and scattered thousands of Africans, including a family named Deah.

trampled, killed, and scattered thousands of Liberians and other Africans, including a family named Deah. Roland was just one very lonely man in one large American city. How many other Liberians lived thousands of miles from their homeland – alone, orphaned, damaged, and hopeless?

The power of empathy brings and bonds people together like no other emotion. Those who have suffered the same injuries can find each other in the vast sea of humanity all around them. So it was for Roland Deah. He met another Liberian refugee in Tucson.

As the two men grew into friendship, Roland learned that "Angelo" sent part of each paycheck to his parents who lived in "Peace Town," the same refugee camp that had been home to Roland almost a decade earlier. Because Roland was an orphan, he decided to support Angelo's parents too. So, he gave cash to Angelo for them.

A month later, Angelo's mother asked if she could speak to Roland; she wanted to know and thank their benefactor. Another month passed before circumstances permitted Roland to take the call from her. After expressing her gratitude, she began to inquire about Roland's life.

"Where did you live in Liberia," she asked.

"Zwedru."

"What tribe are you?"

"Krahn."

"And what is your tribal name?"

"Roland Bello Deah."

She paused.

"Roland, what is your mother's name," she asked slowly.

"Her name was Rebecca, but she died in the civil war," Roland replied.

"And what was your father's name?"

"Brown."

"Oh, my God," she cried.

"What? What?" Roland didn't understand the conversation.

"You are not an orphan. I know your parents!"

Although her report sounded good, Roland was immediately suspicious. Others in the past, motivated by greed, had lied to him with similar reports (he had even sent money to two of them). Roland was concerned that this desperate woman, knowing very well that Roland had money and was generous, had contrived a scheme to extract more money.

"May I talk to my mother," he asked.

The woman told him that she would get his mother; it would take a few days. Roland bought a fifty-dollar phone card and waited for the agreed time. He could not sleep the night before the call.

When the time came, Roland placed the call. He heard a woman's voice, "Hello."

"They tell me that you are my mom."

"Yes, I think so," she hesitated.

"Tell me what you told us after church each Sunday."

"I asked my children to recite a Bible verse from the service in order to make sure that you paid attention to the sermon."

Roland began jumping, crying and shouting. His mother wept softly. He asked her the names of her children. She recited each name, including three that she bore after they were separated.

In that moment, mother and son fell into the unimaginable generosity of the One "who is able to do immeasurably more than all we ask or imagine."[8] The fighting elephants are one version of history. But, another is infinitely larger. As Roland stared at the phone through his tears, he frolicked in that larger story, the too-good-to-be-true narrative of the great Shepherd and Deliverer of the oppressed...Consider the story as told by God to Ezekiel:

> "As a shepherd seeks out his flock...so will I seek out My sheep and deliver them from all the places where they were scattered on a cloudy and dark day...

> "I will seek what was lost and bring back what was driven away, bind up the broken and strengthen what was sick...

> "Behold, I shall judge between sheep and sheep, between rams and goats. Is it too little for you to have eaten up the good pasture, that you must tread down with your feet the residue of your pasture—and to have drunk of the clear waters, that you must foul the residue with your feet?

> "...Because you have pushed with side and shoulder, butted all the weak ones with your horns,

---

8 Ephesians 3:20, taken from the Holy Bible, New International Version®, NIV®. Copyright © 1973, 1978, 1984, 2011 by Biblica, Inc.™ Used by permission of Zondervan. All rights reserved worldwide. www.zondervan.com.

THE DAY OF THE ELEPHANTS

and scattered them abroad, therefore I will save My flock, and they shall no longer be a prey; and I will judge between sheep and sheep...

"I will make a covenant of peace with them, and cause wild beasts to cease from the land; and they will dwell safely in the wilderness and sleep in the woods. I will make them and the places all around My hill a blessing; and I will cause showers to come down in their season; there shall be showers of blessing. Then the trees of the field shall yield their fruit, and the earth shall yield her increase. They shall be safe in their land; and they shall know that I am the LORD, when I have broken the bands of their yoke and delivered them from the hand of those who enslaved them.

And they shall no longer be a prey for the nations, nor shall beasts of the land devour them; but they shall dwell safely, and no one shall make them afraid.[9]"

---

9 Ezekiel 34: 12 - 28, Scripture taken from the New King James Version. Copyright © 1982 by Thomas Nelson, Inc. Used by permission. All rights reserved.

CHAPTER 7

REDEMPTION!

W hen Roland spoke with his father a few days later, he learned more of what happened on September 12, 1990.

Brown and Rebecca, suspecting nothing, had decided to take three-year-old Mona and their infant Patrick with them to their business. After arriving at their store, Rebecca took the children and left, on foot, to open her nearby market.

A few minutes later, Brown heard gunfire. After weeks of rumor, he knew the rebels had arrived. This could be very bad. Brown told Bayee, his employee and brother-in-law, to lock up the store; they were going to the Deah house to check on the family.

A rocket cut Bayee in half; he fell to the dirt dying. Brown screamed and dropped down beside him. There was nothing he could do.

As Brown and Bayee jumped into the pickup to leave, the gunfire got louder. They heard massive explosions and screaming rockets. They drove faster, but as they got close to the Deah house, neighbors came running and told the men to turn around.

"Brown, go back quickly. Men came and killed your family. Please go. It's too dangerous."

He was horrified and numbed by the report, but the rocket barrage ignited survival instincts. As they stood outside the pickup, considering what to do, a rocket cut Bayee in half; he fell to the dirt dying. Brown screamed and dropped down beside him. There was nothing he could do.

With the roads suddenly too dangerous and impassable, Brown abandoned his pickup and began running toward the Prime Timber Production Refugee Camp (the PTP). When he arrived, he frantically clawed through the growing number of people who had fled Zwedru; he had to find his wife and children. After a long search, he saw them! He ran and embraced the only ones he knew were still alive.

Hours later, they – Brown, Rebecca, Mona, and Patrick – joined thousands of others walking toward Ivory Coast. They never saw their home or Zwedru or Liberia again.

As they walked, they prayed and cried. The enormity of loss was crushing. When the sun rose that morning, they had everything they could ever hope to have – fine family, nice home, good cars, successful businesses, money, land, and other possessions. By the time the sun had gone down, they had lost it all. They were refugees, wearing everything they had left. They walked by day and slept by the side of the road at night.

From that day until the day that Roland and his father talked, they had lived in refugee camps or worse. They had not seen a bathroom in all those years. Yet, in the timeless story of the continuation of the species, they produced three more children while living in such squalid circumstances.

Reunion

At the time of their talk, Brown and Rebecca and children lived in the forest. So Roland became very decisive; he told his parents to find a place in the village. He would pay for it. So began the new relationship, the timeless pattern by which children become the protectors of their parents.

Roland was not satisfied with moving his parents to the village; he wanted them to join him in America. In

2007, they started the process that would relocate them to Tucson. He found a resettlement program that would bring his family to the United States. The government would provide it as a loan.

On Thursday evening, September 10, 2009, Roland's phone rang. His father announced, "We're in New York." They would arrive at 3:00 PM the next day. Roland, so excited that he could not sleep, called a Liberian friend. They both jumped into action to cook lots of food for the grand arrival of this family of nine.

At three o'clock the next afternoon, Roland stood in the Tucson airport waiting for his family. The only problem was that no one in the arriving party really knew whom to look for! And the greeter, Roland, couldn't identify his party either. But then Roland saw a family – father and mother and the right number of children – carrying UN refugee bags.

Roland could not speak as he walked toward the family. His arms and spine were chilled. As he got closer, the family began to stare at him. Could he be? Roland? Everyone began to cry. They had not seen each other in almost exactly nineteen years. After nearly two decades of being an "orphan," Roland held his parents, his brothers, and his sisters.

After collecting luggage, they went "home" to Roland's apartment. Roland told me, "We didn't sleep all night. We just talked and told stories upon stories upon stories." Yes, almost twenty years of stories.

Stories of lives lost in Liberia and found in America.

CHAPTER 8

LOSING AND FINDING LIFE

I had listened in rapt, and sometimes tearful, silence for more than two hours. This young African man had ripped the lid off my view of the world.

Although he and I are very different, we are also the same.

We've each lived in our own jungles and faced our own terrors. We each came to the end of our own strength and, in that moment, crashed through into the unfathomable strength and goodness of God.

As a Christian for many years, I realized that this man – about thirty years younger than me – has been broiled in God's oven of suffering and "severe mercies." Like Job, the Deah family knew the tornado that can suck

Like Job, the Deah family knew the tornado that can suck everything away in an instant.

everything away in an instant. I've not lost a fraction of what was taken from them.

Those who experience great loss obtain a great gift of new sight. They can see the higher ground of Heaven clearer than they see the mud ruts of their Earth life. Like those burned at stakes, hung on crosses, mauled by wild animals, and other martyrs throughout history, they can see that Heaven is "right there" – so very near. Just through that membrane.

They see the transcendent reunion with all those who once visited earth in their journey. No wonder John wrote of those who "overcome" because they did not love their lives so much that they were afraid to die."[10]

Death and loss are portals to greater life. Greater life in the care of the everlasting Shepherd, the One Who even attends to the health and well being of ravens and lilies. I remain astonished that God protected one little boy just as He loved, covered, and guided Moses in a basket on a river.

And, how incredible that Roland met one man in Tucson – one person among a million in Pima County

---

10 Revelation 12:11 from the Holy Bible, New Living Translation, copyright ©1996, 2004, 2007 by Tyndale House Foundation. Used by permission of Tyndale House Publishers, Inc., Carol Stream, Illinois 60188. All rights reserved.

– whose mother in Ivory Coast actually knew Roland's parents. She was, in fact, the only link on planet Earth between the members of this scattered family.

That is great, profound, and immeasurable life!

Because of one Liberian man's story, I ended that day with less affection for Earth and its addictions and more trust in the Lord of my life. After all, He said, "For whoever wants to save his life will lose it, but whoever loses his life for me will save it."[11]

This young African man knows, and has taught and continues to teach me, much about life – lost and found.

Roland continues to press the boundaries of his new life in America. He recently walked into my office and – grinning from ear to ear and his eyes brimming with emotion – proudly handed me his U.S. citizenship papers.

I marvel at his excitement in seeking to capture the American dream for himself and his family. And, yet, as we both survey this land that we love, Roland and I see many who are native to this land, but seem to despise

---

11 Luke 9: 24 from the Holy Bible, New International Version®, NIV®. Copyright © 1973, 1978, 1984, 2011 by Biblica, Inc.™ Used by permission of Zondervan. All rights reserved worldwide. www.zondervan.com.

the very dream that has pulled Roland and millions of other immigrants here.

Too many American-born people are uninformed, resentful, ungrateful, and demanding. Something in their heart or brain has been immobilized. It appears that they do not know they can achieve great things.

As I've considered this enigma, I've wondered, is it possible that immigrants (like Roland) may be the seed of a new harvest in America?

According to an old story, in the 1830s a vineyard in France shipped some of its best stock of vines to an American winery. A few years later, the great blight destroyed almost half of Europe's finest wineries. When the blight passed and the soil was cured, the American wine maker sent some of the "immigrant" vines back to France. Today, that vineyard continues to operate because the old vines came back.

When I look at Roland, I see some classic values – derived from old rootstock and cultivated in foreign soil– returning to America.

THROUGH THE EYES OF A STRANGER

Every time Roland talks about America, I hear something fresh. For example, Roland sees America as a verdant "field of dreams" for him and others escaping unspeakable conditions. He sees the vast tapestry of opportunities that still call out to the rest of the world. Compared to what he saw in the unrestrained rape, pillage, and murder that nearly destroyed a nation, what he sees in America is still the glorious "city upon a hill."

Pauline Mujawamariya, the Jewish Family and Children's Service representative who assisted Roland in his resettlement, remembers "his assurance that he would succeed in America. He did not seem needy."

These days I often think that I would love for Roland and other refugees to tell all of us how they see America. Maybe this country needs to see itself through the eyes of immigrants. What if political parties, business groups, Chambers of Commerce, churches, civic organizations, and other associations could listen to those who came here from the faraway places of the earth?

And could native-born Americans begin to see themselves differently? Could they catch a glimpse of America as a land of opportunity, a land that is still the best hope?

For example, Roland is astonished at the breadth and depth of stress in America. He is just incredulous that Americans need medication to get them through their working days. He wonders why "girlfriend stuff, problems at work, and debt" could possibly drive people into stress! This man who lived through human slaughter, watched brutal rapes, dwelled in the squalor and disease of refugee camps, and suffered other horrors (as a child!) cannot understand how people can be driven so deep into the emotional abyss by so little.

Perhaps it would help some Americans to hear him talk about that and other things.

When Roland was a child in Liberia, the concepts of freedom, democracy, respect for individuals, etc. were virtual synonyms for America. And most Liberians knew that! That is why refugees don't make homemade boats to fight their way into China, Chile, or New Zealand. Roland's dream was not to go to France (even though he spoke French) or to any other land. America was the only portal to what his heart reached for.

Incredibly, when I hear Roland talk about America, I hear more of the ancient wisdom (that built America) than I do when many of our elected officials talk.

America's problems may not be as unsolvable as they appear and feel. Maybe we just need new voices and visions that carry timeless wisdom.

Could it be that God – the One Who gave the wisdom upon which America was built – will place it in whatever vessels He chooses? Even if they are strangers to our shores? That has happened innumerable times in our history. Consider Albert Einstein, Andrew Carnegie, Wernher von Braun, and thousands of others who provided a new conduit of wisdom into America.

According to Matthew 11:25, it is God's nature to hide and reveal wisdom however He chooses.

Roland Deah and millions like him may represent new and sparkling streams of wisdom for America's future. America's problems may not be as unsolvable as they appear and feel.

Maybe we just need new voices and visions that carry timeless wisdom.

The Huddled Masses Yearning to Breathe Free

A poem, written by Emma Lazarus, at the base of the statue of liberty contains the famous invitation, "Give me your tired, your poor, your huddled masses yearning to breathe free, the wretched refuse of your teeming shore. Send these, the homeless, tempest-tossed to me, I lift my lamp beside the golden door!"

Those words are being tested today. Because criminals so routinely transgress our borders, many

Americans have been pushed into (very understandable) reaction against all immigrants. But perhaps this is a situation that calls for new eyes.

When Kelly Scherrer, the wife of a U. S. Marine combat pilot, read about Roland she wrote, "Roland's story is the best argument I've seen for pressing into the hard work of maintaining liberty and justice for the homeless and oppressed of the earth. The fact that Roland found refuge here, through a program designed for refugees like him, orphaned and dislocated, is all the testimony I need that America is a country worth fighting for!

"My husband is presently committed to active duty in the Marine Corps. He spent two tours overseas in terrible living conditions, missed out on our son's adoption and two different seasons of major holidays. Furthermore, he lives with the weight of stories he cannot tell and habits he'd rather not have from living with death just one error away. What was all that for? I gain a glimpse of the reason when I read Roland's story.

"Amazingly, America began as a refuge for the oppressed and the abandoned, for the losers and failures who hoped to find a new start in a new land. Starting over is never easy. There's so much lost and so much to be mourned when people leave (or are driven from) their homeland.

"Grief will haunt the refugee for the rest of his days. That grief can cripple him or her in their new land (agencies like the Jewish Family and Children's Service, that helped Roland, can certainly help to lift them over those factors).

"I am so thankful to live and work and fight under the heavy demands of our military operations, if it means creating a refuge for people like Roland. By offering refuge for the oppressed peoples of the earth, we can be a powerful threat to 'the elephants' that trample the grass everywhere.

"We will not run the race in vain, if we can learn to love our neighbors with the respect due to persons. These 'fellow Americans' are our neighbors--whether they've been here for a hundred years or just arrived across the border."

THE DAY OF THE CRAFTSMEN

The whole world has experienced "the day of the elephants." The roaring, rampaging, ruthless beasts trample individuals, families, and communities all over the world.

Every reader of this book has known those enormous

and deadly hooves. I have known those elephants in a physical sense (and also in a modern and western business terrain – that is another story for another book). Roland and millions of other refugees have felt the weight of the elephants in more primitive – and far more dangerous – situations in various lands around the world.

The ancient prophet Zechariah once described a struggle between the "horns" and the "craftsmen."[12] The horns (think: bull elephants) snort, ripple their muscles, and paw the ground. They bellow and impale victims on their horns and toss them around. Their purpose is simply to terrify, disrupt, and scatter.

The bulls are subdued, not by bigger bulls and not by matadors, but by craftsmen. These artisans, perhaps carpenters, eventually drive the bulls away through the quiet and steady rhythms of wisdom and excellence; quality trumps decibels and commotion.

The old prophet could see the sound and fury that agitate and destabilize society. But, more importantly, he also saw the consistent, often unnoticed, craftsmanship that forges community.

Another prophet's vision – presented at the very beginning of this book – remains true and inevitable.

_____

12   Zechariah 1: 18 - 21

History's savage beasts are doomed. The slave masters will be shackled and carried away. The rogue and criminal nations will be destroyed. The Roland Deahs of the earth will live in safety.

And no one will make them afraid.

Roland Deah, 2012